THE CLEAR AND PRESENT TRUTH OF
666

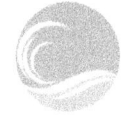

Rapid Movements Publishing

Copyright © 2021 by Tory St.Cyr

Second Edition

All Rights Reserved

Published by Rapid Movements Publishing
Hampton, GA 30228

Other books by Tory St.Cyr may be purchased at theadventistwatchman.com

The author assumes full responsibility for the accuracy of all facts and quotations, as cited in this book.

ISBN: 978-0-578-84574-6

This book is dedicated to one of my closest friends, Jamaar Braswell. You were the first person who came to my mind when God revealed this truth to me. Thank you for picking up the phone and just listening to me ramble about 666. You were my first level of feedback to this truth and well-deserving of this dedication.

Contents

Preface 9
Chapter 1 - The Legend of 666 11
Chapter 2 - The Journey Begins 17
   Other Scriptures that refer to 666 18
   Our Books 19
   Vicarius Filii Dei 21
   Gematria 24
      Nimrod 28
      Caesar Nero 29
      Mankind 30
      Nebuchadnezzar 31
   A made-up number! 35
Chapter 3 - Three Simple Rules 37
      The Dragon 43
      The Beast 47
      The False Prophet 52
   Ellen White and the Three-fold Union 58
   Restating the Three Rules 63
Chapter 4 - The Biblical Meaning of 666 65
   Here is Wisdom 66
   The Seven Mountains 68
   The Beast that Was, Is Not, Yet Is 73
   A Short Space 74
   The Eighth King 76
   The Number of the Beast 78
   Great Babylon's Number 79
   666 is now made up 86
Chapter 5 - Questions and Objections 89
Test your knowledge 97
Topical index 109

Preface

I have always desired to understand the meaning of 666. This desire led me to attend multiple Revelation seminars and study numerous books on the subject. However, I never felt satisfied with any of the explanations I received. I began asking God if there was another interpretation of 666 that was simple to understand and could be taught straight from the Bible.

After much prayer and fasting, the Lord answered my prayer! One bright and sunny morning, the Lord gave me the understanding of 666 that I had been asking for! That morning, God revealed to me that 666 is more than a number—it is a message for these last days! Once I understood the meaning and message behind 666, I decided to write this book for others searching for this same truth.

If you are looking for the true meaning of 666, then this book is for you. This book will take you through my experience with God and the process of discovering the true meaning behind 666. I am confident that once you get to the end of this book, you will realize, just like I did, that most of us have been overlooking the obvious. The meaning of 666 has been right before our eyes this whole time, and John the Revelator was not trying to hide it.

If the meaning of 666 is still a mystery to you, then I hope the explanation found on the pages of this book brings you clarity. Once you understand the Clear and Present Truth of 666, I can all but guarantee that you will never view prophecy the same again.

Chapter 1

The Legend of 666

> "Here is wisdom. Let him that hath understanding count the number of the beast: for it is the number of a man; and his number is Six hundred threescore and six." Revelation 13:18

I think it is safe to say that in the history of humanity, no number has ever struck us with as much intrigue, superstition, and straight-up fear as this mysterious number that John the Revelator calls the number of the Beast. Christians and unbelievers are generally at odds regarding anything of faith and morality; however, we all appear to be on the same page when it comes to this one number. Believers and unbelievers, Christians and Atheists, religious and non-religious, are all on one accord! All are saying the same thing! All with the same general belief! What belief is this, you might ask? The belief that 666 is inherently an evil number. The belief that forbids us from having any association with these three numbers or face severe consequences.

I can recall working as a drive-through cashier at a popular fast-food restaurant in my mid-teens. One day, a middle-aged man, after making his order over the speaker, drove around to my window so he could pay for his meal. Everything was routine at this point, except for the fact that he seemed hesitant to pay for the food that he had just ordered.

He said to me, "Can you repeat my order?"

"Sure," I replied, "You ordered two burgers, a large fry, a small fry, and a small soda."

It was a simple order, so I wasn't quite sure why he seemed indecisive.

Then he brought his face closer to my window as if he were about to tell me something huge. I attentively waited. Was he a government defector about to give me the US nuclear launch codes? Maybe he worked at Area 51, and I was about to know all about those aliens.

But no. This man looked me in the eye and said, "Now can you repeat my total?"

What a total letdown! As I realized this was not my debut as a secret agent spy for a covert government operation, I let out a huge sigh of disappointment...in my mind.

"Your total? Sure." I said, stumbling through my words, trying to provide him with the best customer service experience even though my spirits were a little crushed.

I quickly looked down at the big, clunky metal box called a cash register (Am I revealing my age?), and at the top right-hand corner, there was his total.

I looked back at the customer, as he seemed to be anxious. This was the moment he had been waiting for, and it was my duty not to disappoint.

"Ok," I began, "your total is $6.66." Yes, I was slightly proud of my prompt delivery of a customer's inquiry. And yes, I mentally patted myself on the back.

At that point, I held out my hand with the expectation that he would place something in my hand called cash (Yes, I am anticipating one day readers will not know what this is), but as I looked at this man, he was not getting the money out of his wallet. As a matter of fact, he appeared under duress...even frightened.

He then said to me, "You're going to have to add something to my order."

I was not catching on, and I responded accordingly. "Why, did I miss something?"

He then laughed as if I was oblivious to a glaringly obvious issue.

"What?" I responded, slightly curious and slightly offended. Now the tables had turned, and I was the one getting anxious and filled with anticipation.

"Well," he began (and I guess now was the moment I had been waiting for), "Uh, there's just no way I'm going to allow my total to be 666!"

OH! I finally understood! He believed something sinister would happen to him if I allowed his total to remain at $6.66!

How could I not have known? I hastily pushed another button on my register and looked back at the man. "Sir, would you like sprinkles on that sundae?"

Ladies and Gentlemen, make no mistake about it; there are thousands, maybe hundreds of thousands of people that are just like this man; they will go to any lengths to avoid 666, even adding a hot fudge sundae to an order (with sprinkles on top).

But there is also a flip side to this; there is another extreme. You see, sometimes this mysterious number produces the opposite effect. Some are running towards this number instead of running away from it.

There are those in our society who personify this number *because* they worship Satan. Sometimes it is covertly displayed by popular singers and musicians who attempt to hide this number in plain sight on their album covers or use hand gestures that symbolize it. Yet, there are other musicians who are not trying to hide it and even name their songs after the mysterious number. My point here is that, at its best, many of us attribute this number to bad luck, but often 666 is thought to be synonymous with wickedness, demonic possession, and ultimately Satan himself. However, it should be noted that nowhere in Scripture does the Bible say 666 is the number of Satan. Scripture tells us that 666 is the number of the Beast! And so, the legend of 666 continues to grow.

Now, I would like to pose a simple question to you as the reader: Is it possible that we have entirely misunderstood the meaning and purpose of 666? I had to ask myself this same question, and when I did, I discovered something that I never noticed before. However, before you find out what that is, you first must understand the background of how and why I began the journey to find out the true meaning of 666. You need to know how my journey began.

Chapter 2

The Journey Begins

Several years ago, I planned a prophecy seminar for my church in Orlando, Florida. I remember sitting down to ensure that I was covering all the topics that are typically deemed necessary for a presentation on end-time events. I compiled a mental checklist of all the material that I believed the audience would expect me to cover. The mental checklist started like this:

> Wars and rumors of wars? Check
> Famines? Check
> False Christs? Check
> Mark of the Beast? Check

I am sure you get the picture by now. However, as I got to the end of this mental checklist, I realized one component was omitted. People would definitely want to know the meaning of 666. I mean, how can anyone do a prophecy presentation and fail to mention 666, right? So I decided to incorporate 666 into the program, but there was one problem—I did not fully understand the meaning of 666. How could I teach what I did not understand myself?

As a student of the Bible, I learned that scriptures are the best interpreters of other scriptures. In other words, to understand the meaning of a text or phrase in the Bible, the best places to look for clarity are other scriptures in the Bible. If the meaning of 666 was revealed, I concluded that the Word of God would be its revealer.

Other Scriptures that refer to 666

I began this journey by searching every reference in the Bible that contained the number 666. My search initially took me to the book of Ezra. In listing the exiles taken to Babylon by King Nebuchadnezzar, the Jewish scribe documented the groups and the number of people within those groups. He wrote,

> "The children of Adonikam, six hundred sixty and six." Ezra 2:13

Hmmm...maybe this was the man that the Bible talked about in Revelation 13. I attempted to study a little more about Adonikam to determine if there was anything unique about him. However, after studying this for a couple of days, I realized there simply wasn't enough information about Adonikam in Scripture for me to formulate any type of sound doctrine. I could not find the link between his name and the apocalyptic number that struck fear in the hearts of men and women around the world. So I did what most rational human beings would do in this situation—I moved on.

To my delight, there was another Scriptural reference to 666, which says,

> "Now the weight of gold that came to Solomon in one year was six hundred

threescore and six talents of gold."
1Kings 10:14

Aha! It must be this amount of gold that came to Solomon! We all know Solomon had issues. Could he be the man spoken of in Revelation 13? If so, how did those issues relate to 666? More importantly, why would God give Solomon all that wisdom and then reduce his name to the number of the Beast in Revelation 13? I couldn't accept this belief, and so I decided to move on once again.

Unfortunately, I wasn't able to find any other direct references to the number 666 in the Word of God, and I must admit, I was slightly disappointed that I seemed to have hit a roadblock so early in my journey.

It was at this moment that I had an epiphany. I remembered that the Seventh-day Adventist Church does focus a lot of attention on prophecy. It would only be reasonable for the explanation of 666 to be written in one of our books! So, for the next step of my journey, I decided to study as many Adventist books on prophecy as I could get my hands on. I was confident that with the array of books and articles written by Adventist scholars, I would eventually find a reasonable interpretation of 666 that would satisfy the current prophetic void that I was experiencing. Yes! It must be in one of our books.

Our Books

Growing up in the Seventh-day Adventist church, I can remember going to many Daniel and Revelation seminars, and I can specifically recall a few preachers mentioning 666 in their sermons. Yes, it was all coming back to me. I knew this was taught in many of our churches, but I couldn't remember what exactly was said.

I began searching for some documentation written by Adventist authors. I turned to my bookshelf, which was packed with all types of books written by Adventist authors and Bible scholars. I allowed my eyes to pan the list of titles until something would catch my eye. My eyes panned a book on the Second Coming—but that probably wouldn't mention 666. I then saw a book about healthy eating; however, unless 666 was a piece of fruit, I'm not sure it would contain any references to the number of the Beast.

Then I saw it! Uriah Smith's *Daniel and the Revelation*! I picked it up and opened it to the index, and sure enough, 666 was right there waiting for me! I quickly sat down, ready to take notes in order to make my presentation complete. I couldn't turn the pages fast enough. I wanted to enjoy this, so I got up from my office chair and sat down on the futon that aligned the back wall of my small home office. I had a notebook in hand, ready to take down all the necessary notes. I turned to the indicated page and began to read. On page 624, it reads:

> "The most plausible expression we have seen suggested as containing the number of the beast, is the title which the pope takes to himself, and allows others to apply to him. That title is this: Vicarious Filli Dei, "Vicegerent of the Son of God." Taking the letters out of this title which the Latins used as numerals, and giving them their numerical value, we have just 666."[1]

---

[1] Uriah Smith, Daniel and the Revelation 1909, p. 624

Vicarius Filii Dei

Essentially, Uriah Smith was suggesting that 666 was a number that was attributed to the Pope. He suggests that the pontiff wore a crown or tiara during the Middle Ages, which had the title, "Vicarius Filii Dei," inscribed on it. This Latin phrase means *representative of the Son of God*.

According to this author, each letter of Vicarius Filii Dei is transliterated into Roman numerals, and those Roman numerals add up to 666 as shown below:

V	5	F	0	D	500
I	1	I	1	E	0
C	100	L	50	I	1
A	0	I	1		+ 501
R	0	I	1		
I	1		+ 53		
U	5				= 666
S	0				
	112				

What many Seventh-day Adventists are unaware of is that the early Adventists did not teach Vicarius Filii Dei as the meaning of 666. The early pioneers taught that 666 was a reference to Protestantism in the United States. Here are a few references:

> "They are harlots because of their intercourse with the man of sin. And their number is the number of a man, (the man of sin,) and his

number is six hundred three score and six. Those churches collectively or individually have that number...Hence the number of his name, the church represented by him is, 666; and this is the number of every division of that church, and of every member belonging thereto; hence the number is coupled with the mark and the name of the beast, as a matter of equal importance, and as involving the same consequences."[2]

"We may trace the lineage of every Protestant church back to the mother of harlots, and we can go no farther. Not only are they daughters by natural descent, but by imitation. And their number is the number of a man, (the man of sin,) and his number is six hundred three score and six. Those churches collectively or individually, have that number."[3]

So, if the correlation of the number 666 to the phrase "Vicarius Filii Dei" did not originate with the Seventh-day Adventist Church, how did our church arrive at this interpretation? According to LeRoy Froom, the idea of correlating 666 to Vicarius Filii Dei was believed to have originated in the early 17th century by Andreas Helwig, a Protestant Christian author. In Helwig's book *Antichristus Romanus,* Froom says that Helwig emphasized Vicarius Filii Dei as the Pope's title and noted that 666 was its numerical calculation.[4] From my

---

[2] James White, The Advent Review, and Sabbath Herald, vol. 4 p. 166 (1853)
[3] J.N. Loughborough - The Two Horned Beast, p. 47 (1854)
[4] The Prophetic Faith of Our Fathers, vol. 2 pg. 606

research, it appears that Stephen Haskell and Uriah Smith would eventually use their writings to push Helwig's interpretation to their readers. Ultimately, Seventh-day Adventists would eventually adopt this interpretation as part of our unofficial belief system, and the rest is history.

Now that we've deviated to establish some historical context, let's go back to my office with me sitting on the futon. I now understood what 666 meant. I was good, right? I wrote down all the points that I would make regarding Vicarius Filii Dei and even added a slide to my presentation showing how to calculate 666. I then decided I would show my audience examples of a Pope displaying this title on his crown. However, to my surprise, I could not find any photos or paintings of the Pope's crown showing this title. How strange was that? I scoured the internet looking for any official documentation in order to prove that Vicarius Filii Dei was the Pope's official title. However, I was only able to find a handful of historical references to this title.

Maybe it was just me, but I felt that if Vicarius Filii Dei was truly the name of the Beast that God warns us to avoid in Revelation 13, that this truth would be a little more evident than the sporadic documentation found online. It seemed to me that this number should be recognizable to anyone living in the modern world without having to obtain never-before-seen top-secret documentation.

Then, the thought occurred to me: Even if I were able to prove that some Popes wore this title, that doesn't prove that this is the meaning of 666 in the book of Revelation. Now, don't get me wrong. I fully believe that at some point in history, a few Popes did wear a crown that had Vicarius Filii Dei inscribed on it, but at the end of the day, all it proves is that some Popes wore this title. In other words, there is a limitless supply of words, phrases, and titles that add up to 666. The proof of the Pope wearing one of those titles is not enough to uproot any other titles without a strong system of Biblical interpretation to accompany that proof. Thus, the more I studied Vicarius Filii Dei, the more I realized this was not the meaning of 666.

I want to point out that I have known and still know people who believe 666 refers to Vicarius Filii Dei. As a matter of fact, you may get to the end of this book and maintain your original belief of 666—and this is Ok. How we interpret 666 doesn't appear to be a salvific issue, and I have no animosity toward individuals who embrace differing viewpoints. As for me, I was convinced Vicarius Filii Dei was not the meaning of 666, especially when I discovered something called Gematria.

Gematria

In my research, I discovered that the method used to convert Vicarius Filii Dei to 666 is called "Gematria." Ladies and Gentlemen, I suggest you do your own research on gematria and allow the Holy Spirit to lead and guide you. However, here is how the American Heritage Dictionary defines it:

> **Gematria**: A numerological system used in kabbalah and other forms of Jewish mysticism that assigns numerical values

to words based on the fixed numerical values of their letters.[5]

Now, in the above statement, there are three words that should concern you:

1. Numerological (Numerology)
2. Kabbalah
3. Mysticism

I will define these words, and I would like you to decide if any of them are a conflict of interest with Christianity.

I will take each one individually:

> **Numerology**: The study of the occult significance of numbers.[6]

For those who are not aware, believers should have nothing to do with occult-related practices; this is Satan's territory.

It is crazy to think that we are only on the first word, and already we are on Satan's ground. But we cannot stop here; let us look at the second word:

> **Kabbalah**: A body of mystical teachings of rabbinical origin, often based on an esoteric interpretation of the Hebrew Scriptures.[7]

---

[5] American Heritage® Dictionary of the English Language, Fifth Edition.
[6] "Numerology." Merriam-Webster.com Dictionary, Merriam-Webster, https://www.merriam-webster.com/dictionary/numerology.
[7] American Heritage® Dictionary of the English Language, Fifth Edition.

Are you seeing this? While I shouldn't have to go to the last word, I will do it so there is no doubt in your mind what we are associating with when we use gematria to derive Biblical doctrine.

> **Mysticism**: the doctrine of an immediate spiritual intuition of truths believed to transcend ordinary understanding, or of a direct, intimate union of the soul with God through contemplation or spiritual ecstasy.[8]

How ironic! As Seventh-day Adventists, we condemn Sunday sanctification because of its connection to sun worship. So on the one hand, we condemn Paganism, and then on the other hand use Mysticism to interpret 666. Do you see the irony? Now ask yourself this question: Why would God command us to abstain from spiritualism in all its forms but require us to use spiritualism to obtain this particular teaching of prophecy from Revelation? Paul said,

> "...what fellowship hath righteousness with unrighteousness? and what communion hath light with darkness." 2 Corinthians 6:14

It was clear to me that while Vicarius Filii Dei worked for some, my conscience would not allow it to work for me, and therefore, I had to reject it as part of my belief system.

---

[8] Random House Kernerman Webster's College Dictionary, © 2010 K Dictionaries Ltd.

So now what? I knew that I did not want to hold a prophecy seminar and omit mentioning 666, but how could I make a presentation when I was clueless on the topic? Then a light bulb went off in my head. Of course! I will get my understanding of 666 from the best repository known to man—the Internet! (Did you just laugh?)

The Internet

From what I have been told, this world has around seven billion people living in it. Out of the seven billion people, I believed someone knew the meaning of 666 and placed that information on the internet. All I needed to do was find its location.

So, in the interest of full disclosure, for six months, I only studied 666. Morning devotions, Sabbath school lessons, and evening worship were all hijacked by 666 research. Even my prayers all sounded like this: "Dear Heavenly Father, thank you for this day. Lord, thank you for waking me up. Now, Father, please tell me what 666 means today! Lord, we want the same thing...to let your truth be known. Please reveal it to me today. In Jesus' name. Amen."

At this point, I want to apologize to anyone who, during this time, asked me to pray for them, and I was so obsessed with 666 that I completely forgot to mention their name in my prayers. Charge it to my head, not to my heart.

So, my spare time was spent looking for that one soul among the seven billion that had been given the understanding of 666. I scoured the internet and popular video hosting sites in my quest to understand this mystery. I would even go to sleep listening to YouTube videos, hoping that something would tap into my subconscious and I would miraculously wake up with this knowledge. I took in as much as I could from the online communities. Here are just a few of the ideas that I remember listening to regarding the meaning of 666:

Nimrod, who is considered by many to be the father of Mystery Religions[9], is a popular choice for many 666 enthusiasts, and honestly, it makes a lot of sense. Think about it this way:
- The Bible says he was a mighty one upon the earth (Gen 10:8).
- It also says that he was the one who built Babel (Gen 10:10).
- The Tower of Babel was the scene upon which God confounded the world's languages (Gen 11:19); therefore, Babel, which Babylon is derived from, is synonymous with confusion.

So the person who started the mystery religions also built Babylon and happened to be a man. Wow! Talk about a smoking gun, right? Well, I wouldn't consider this an exact slam dunk just yet. Remember, Revelation 13:18 says, "...*Let him that hath understanding count the number of the beast...*" This theory claims the Beast is Rome (which I happen to agree with), but my question is, what did Nimrod have to do with Rome? Rome was Pagan from its inception, but so were all the other world powers before Rome. What made Rome so connected with

---

[9] Alexander Hislop, The Two Babylons p. 20,22

Nimrod that God would have John emphasize a connection with the Babel builder over all other Pagan nations? I couldn't quite conclude that Nimrod was the name that Revelation referred to for the calculation of 666. Unfortunately, Nimrod was not the smoking gun I thought it was. It felt like it was more smoke than gun. I decided I would move on.

Caesar Nero was a popular choice among Evangelical Christians as the man whose name could be behind this 666 mystery. In my research, I discovered what made Nero a popular choice:
- He was a Roman Emperor
- He persecuted the Christians
- Using gematria, his name adds up to 666.[10]

This theory was conceivable because Nero was a Roman Emperor, and it was logical that a persecutor of God's people would get the attention of the Christian world.

Unfortunately, logic doesn't always equate to Bible truth. John wrote Revelation around 95 AD; however, Nero died in 68 AD.[11] [12] If John were warning believers about Nero, this would mean he was warning believers about an emperor who had been dead for almost thirty years!

Some have suggested that Revelation was written around the time of Nero. If this were the case, we then

---

[10] Using Aramaic
[11] Nero Roman Emperor, Encyclopædia Britannica, online https://www.britannica.com/biography/Nero-Roman-emperor
[12] Pheme Perkins, Reading the New Testament: An Introduction pg. 19

must ask the question: If John knew 666 related to Nero, why wouldn't he mention the emperor by name? Was John's pen low on ink that he couldn't write something like, "The name of the Beast is Nero, whose number is 666?" Some have suggested that John was trying to hide the fact that he was talking about Nero. But why would he? John was already banished to the isle of Patmos for his faith, and I'm not sure mentioning a dead emperor would have made his life any worse. I couldn't make Nero fit the equation. He was not the answer to the 666 question, and so I decided to move on.

Mankind was also identified as the meaning of 666. This theory suggests that when Revelation 13:18 declares, "666 is the number of a man," it's referring to "mankind" because Adam and Eve were created on the sixth day. I found this concept to be somewhat clever. It is derived directly from the Bible, plus it involves the number six.

The problem I have with this theory is that the other 65 books of the Bible already highlight man's sinfulness. It feels somewhat anticlimactic for John to prophesy about the Dragon, the woman, and the Mark of the Beast, then conclude that all was the result of mankind, which was created on the sixth day.

But even if you get past that hurdle, another one exists. Almost every Bible translation refers to the man of Revelation 13:18 as a specific person, not the collective human race. Translators are not infallible, but here, I believe they are correct—this is a specific man.

Finally, the last issue is the biggest. This theory begs the question: Why does Revelation mention three sixes? This theory does not match, as man was created on the sixth day, not the 666th day.

The mankind-is-666 theory does have some logic to it, but not enough logic for me to abandon all other possibilities and anoint this belief as the undisputed champion of 666 theories. Therefore, I decided to move on.

Nebuchadnezzar was also mentioned as the man behind 666. I went to the Book of Daniel and read the following:

> "Nebuchadnezzar the king made an image of gold, whose height was threescore cubits, and the breadth thereof six cubits: he set it up in the plain of Dura, in the province of Babylon."
> Daniel 3:1

A few verses later, it says,

> "That at what time ye hear the sound of the cornet, flute, harp, sackbut, psaltery, dulcimer, and all kinds of musick, ye fall down and worship the golden image that Nebuchadnezzar the king hath set up."
> Daniel 3:5

In the above verses, we see that Nebuchadnezzar's statue was six cubits wide and 60 cubits high, and then later, we see six instruments mentioned as their call to bow down to the idol. So we see three sixes mentioned in this chapter.

It is interesting, but I'm not sure this correlates to the Beast of Revelation 13, as these numbers do not add up to 666. The numbers are actually 6 + 60 + 6. Considering the measurements and the instruments do not add up, this theory is a stretch at best, and I only accept stretches when waking up or before I work out. So, as you probably guessed, I moved on.

I continued my search, but the suggestions became more and more unrealistic, and by this time, my disappointment became evident.

My prayers turned into bribes. I found myself saying things like, "Father, if I don't understand the meaning of 666, I guess I will have to cancel that Daniel and Revelation seminar." I am so glad that God winks at our ignorance.

By this time, my resources were drying up. I was unable to find a satisfactory explanation of 666 from the Scriptures, Adventist books, or the internet.

However, there was one more source that I had not fully explored. While this source was also a Seventh-day Adventist author, I excluded her books from the previous list because I've never heard anyone quote this particular author when it came to the number 666. Her name is Ellen G White. She is considered God's Messenger to the Seventh-day Adventist Church, who I believe had the gift of prophecy.

It is your prerogative to believe her words or to reject them. However, this book's stance on Ellen White is that her writings, while not on par with the Bible, are a source of authoritative commentary on the Bible.

Since I had never read one book that mentioned Ellen White when it came to understanding the meaning of 666, I just assumed she was silent on the issue. I thought that if Ellen White had something to say about 666, surely our books would all quote her, right?

So, I began searching the writings of Ellen White, expecting my search to come up empty. However, I was pleasantly surprised to discover that Ellen White did mention the infamous number on one occasion. However, once I read this quote, I understood why none of our speakers and authors referred to it. I read the quote seven or eight times, but I couldn't believe what I was reading. Here's what she said:

> "I saw all that "would not receive the mark of the Beast, and of his Image, in their foreheads or in their hands," could not buy or sell. I saw that the number (666) of the Image Beast was made up."[13]

When I read this quote, my mouth hit the floor. All the time spent searching the Word of God, reading Adventist authors, searching online resources, and you mean to tell me that 666 is a made-up number? This means John the Revelator, after seeing all of this in vision, decided to make up a number that would represent the name of the Beast. Words cannot express the disbelief and utter disappointment I felt at that very moment. I closed Ellen White's book. I closed the other books, and I even closed my Bible. For the next two weeks, I barely prayed and read Scripture even less. I started this journey by asking God, which turned into begging God, which turned into bribing God, and now I

---

[13] Ellen White, A Word to the Little Flock, P. 19

was ignoring God. In essence, I became a type of Jonah. You know him. He's the guy who so badly wanted Nineveh to be destroyed that he sat on a hill and pouted. Yeah, that guy was me for about two weeks. I was angry at Ellen White for making, what I believed at that time, was an irresponsible statement. I was mad at God for sending me on what I felt was a wild goose chase, and the goose did not even exist. And I may have even snapped at my wife a few times. (Thank God she forgave me)

I felt that there was no reasonable explanation for 666. It seemed odd for God to place something so obscure in such a pivotal chapter of the Bible without giving us more information. It seemed like God was leading me on.

And just to be clear, I am not suggesting or recommending that anyone treat God as I did during this period of my life. I was emotional and became borderline angry with God. He didn't owe me anything, and I had no basis for my attitude toward Him. However, I must say that I am so glad that He was patient with me and taught me to be patient with him. This patience would later prove to be helpful in future books that I would write. Whenever I experienced difficulty understanding Biblical truth, I knew that God (if it was His will) would bless me with the understanding in His time, not mine. Now don't get sentimental on me; this ride is about to get wild, and I need your mind, not your emotions.

So, as I said, for two weeks I did minimal studying or praying. I was practically on strike. However, even during my protest, I kept thinking about 666 being a made-up number.

A made-up number!

After two weeks of being on a spiritual strike, something amazing happened. One Sunday morning, my wife was downstairs doing her usual morning routine, which consisted of washing dishes and cooking breakfast for the family. As I was waking from sleep, I realized something was different. I seemed to be stuck between sleep and awake. Even though I've had this happen before, this time was different. While I was in this trance-like state, the phrase "666 is made-up" kept playing over and over in my head. You see, before this, I kept thinking of that phrase, but this time the phrase seemed to be playing in my head, and I couldn't stop it from repeating. It was as if the words were not coming from me. It felt like someone was repeating them to me. But it wasn't just that...the words seemed to get louder and louder.

Then, as I was lying in bed, it was as if God began downloading information into my head. The best way I can describe this is like a puzzle. All the information I had studied were the little puzzle pieces. I had all the necessary pieces to complete the puzzle, but I just needed someone to start putting the puzzle together. It was as if all the information that I had studied was being rearranged in my head so that I could make sense of it. It was as if God was saying, "OK, you've waited long enough. Here you go."

I immediately jumped up and ran to the dresser next to my bed, found a sticky pad, and began writing down what God was placing into my mind at that moment. I wasn't quite sure what was happening.

Then my eyes were opened. Of course! How did I miss this? All the Revelation seminars I attended. All the studies on prophecy I had taken. Everything I thought I knew about 666 eluded this one simple point: 666 is a made-up number!

The understanding of 666 is so simple that most people are overlooking it! It's like everyone is trying to play Chess when in fact, the game is Checkers!

As a child, I can remember looking for a lost toy in our house, not realizing that the toy was right in front of me. My mom would often say, "If it had been a snake, it would've bit you." In other words, whatever I was looking for was so close in proximity to me that it could have literally touched me. The meaning of 666 is like that toy; it's right in front of you, and John the Revelator is not even trying to mask its meaning.

God jump-started this puzzle, and it was at that moment that I realized I had read the meaning of 666, but it never crossed my mind that that was the meaning of 666! How in the world did I miss this?

Now, as you read the remaining chapters of this book, one of two things will be true:

1. You have never seen what I am about to show you.
2. You've seen it, but never correlated it to 666.

Either way, I hope you read this next chapter thoroughly. The way that I've decided to show this to you is through three simple rules.

Chapter 3

Three Simple Rules

I have discovered that in order to understand the meaning of 666, you must first understand three simple rules. If you can comprehend these three rules and can count to six, then I believe you will realize that 666 is an important message for today. Here are the three rules:

1: A man isn't always a man.

Now, I want you to think about this point. Ask yourself— Is a woman always a woman in Bible prophecy? No. As an Adventist, you should understand that a woman in Bible prophecy typically represents a church. Now, if a woman doesn't always represent a woman, why do you believe a man in Bible prophecy always represents a man?

It is imperative that you understand that when you are reading the Bible, and you come across a Scripture that contains the word "man," "he," or "his," it's not always a flesh and blood man. To be honest with you, this one simple fact and misapplication of this one point has caused most believers to completely misunderstand the meaning of 666. God revealed to me that this was my first problem; I was under the impression that when the Bible says, "*it is the number of a man*," it had to be a flesh-and-blood man.

For those who currently hold a similar viewpoint, my message to you is this: If your interpretation of 666 begins with the belief that the number of a man is a literal man, you are already operating under false pretenses, and these false pretenses will produce a domino effect, skewing your overall outcome. I am not trying to be offensive—just honest.

Generally speaking, most Christians that I've spoken with (Adventists and Non-Adventists alike) believe that the Antichrist is a literal man. While I now disagree with this position, I do understand the logic behind it. It's not beyond the pale for someone to read what the Bible says about the Antichrist and interpret him as a literal man. Notice what John says about the Antichrist in 1 John 2:22:

> "...**He** is antichrist, that denieth the Father and the Son."

Notice what Paul says in 2 Thessalonians 2:3:

> "...that **man** of sin be revealed, the son of perdition."

Daniel follows this same theme in Daniel 7:8.

> "...in this horn were eyes like the eyes of **man**, and a mouth speaking great things."

Do you see it? Everywhere we look, the AntiChrist is personified as a man. He is identified as a "he," or "him," or a "son." But even in the midst of all of this evidence, I stand firm in my declaration to you that this is not a man.

The question now is—What does a man represent in Bible prophecy? Well, when we look at the Scriptures, we discover that God has revealed it to us. In Deuteronomy 28, God referred to the nation that would come against the Children of Israel. Notice how God described this nation:

> "The LORD shall bring a **nation** against thee from far, from the end of the earth, as swift as the eagle flieth; a nation whose tongue thou shalt not understand; A **nation** of fierce countenance, which shall not regard the person of the old, nor shew favour to the young." Deuteronomy 28:49-50

Clearly, we can see that God is referring to a nation. However, notice how the next verse refers to this power:

> "And **HE** shall eat the fruit of thy cattle, and the fruit of thy land, until thou be destroyed: which also shall not leave thee either corn, wine, or oil, or the increase of thy kine, or flocks of thy sheep, until **HE** have destroyed thee." Deuteronomy 28:51

Did you see where God referred to this nation as a man? Thus, we can see that, prophetically, a man can refer to a nation or political entity.

Let's look at another example. Ezekiel 30:24 says, *"And I will strengthen the arms of the king of Babylon, and put my sword in his hand: but I will break Pharaoh's arms, and he shall groan before him with the groanings of a deadly wounded **man**."* Although "man" was added by the translators, we can see that it was correctly supplied, as God clearly personified the Egyptian Empire as a man.

Notice Daniel 7:17 says, "*These great beasts, which are four, are four kings, which shall arise out of the earth.*" We know that a Beast represents a nation, but here, God calls a nation a king, and what gender is a king? A king is a male. Thus, we can see that a woman represents the church, and a man represents the state. And when there is a union of Church and State, it is symbolized as a marriage between the two.

2: Spiritual Babylon is Satan's trinity

The next thing that God revealed to me was something that I had already known but didn't fully understand its significance. That is, the Devil has a trinity.

You see, I always knew that the Devil had a trinity, but I never understood it the way God revealed it to me that morning. When God helped me understand this important truth, I began to see the Devil's trinity in a whole new light—an entirely new perspective. This same perspective is what I am about to give you.

First, let's establish the definition of "trinity." Merriam-Webster states the following:

> The unity of Father, Son, and Holy Spirit as three persons in one Godhead[14]

---

[14] Merriam-Webster.com Dictionary, s.v. "Trinity," accessed August 2, 2020, https://www.merriam-webster.com/dictionary/Trinity.

At our core, Seventh-day Adventists believe in this Three-in-One aspect of God. However, if you are paying close attention, you may be shocked to see that some of our Seventh-day Adventist brethren are questioning if the Holy Spirit is a personal being. This has resulted in a push to move away from the Trinity doctrine.

While I am not fully up to speed with the intricacies of the Non-Trinitarian approach, I do know, from personal interaction, that a number of our people no longer embrace this doctrine as part of their belief system.

Understand that this book's goal is not to persuade or dissuade you in any particular direction regarding the Trinity. What I am about to tell you is not dependent on whether you believe that the Father, Son, and Holy Spirit are three individuals operating in unison, or whether you believe that the Holy Spirit is just the essence of God. You don't have to believe in the Trinity, but you do need to *understand* the Trinity. I'm not necessarily speaking about the Trinity of the Father, Son, and Holy Spirit; I am talking about the three powers that have been utilized by Satan for thousands of years to destroy God's people. The Lord revealed to me that, just as the Father, Son, and Holy Spirit operate as one, Satan's three powers also work as one.

Now, I'm going to say this one more time, because if this does not make sense to you, then the remainder of this book will not make sense. Listen to what I'm telling you as I repeat it: Satan's trinity consists of three individual powers, but these three powers operate as one power. These powers are outlined very carefully in Scripture, and now I will reveal them to you and then prove to you that they are, in fact, three separate powers that work as one power.

The Devil's trinity is found in Revelation 16:13. It reads as follows:

> "And I saw <u>three</u> unclean spirits like frogs come out of the mouth of the **DRAGON**, and out of the mouth of the **BEAST**, and out of the mouth of the **FALSE PROPHET**."

The Dragon, the Beast, and the False Prophet are the three powers that have been, are being, and will continue to be utilized by Satan to destroy God's people.

Now, the logical question is, what do the Dragon, Beast, and False Prophet represent? I could quickly answer this question in one brief sentence, but doing it that way may bring about more questions than answers. Instead of telling you about it, I prefer you to see it yourself. So, what I want you to do is open a Bible and read Revelation 12 and 13. (Yes, all of chapters 12 and 13.)

Ok, assuming that you read the full chapters of Revelation 12 and 13, I want to make sure you understand what you just read. You see, Revelation 12 and 13 are essentially the biographies of the Dragon, the Beast, and the False Prophet. I sometimes even refer to these two chapters as the gospel of the Dragon, Beast, and False Prophet, as these two chapters in Revelation appear to chronicle the careers and agendas of these three entities.

You see, just like Matthew, Mark, Luke, and John tell the story of Christ from their personal vantage points, Revelation 12 and 13 tell the story of the Dragon,

Beast, and False Prophet from each of their vantage points as well.

Revelation 12 tells their story from the vantage point of the Dragon.

Revelation 13:1-10 tells their story from the vantage point of the Beast.

Revelation 13:11-17 tells their story from the vantage point of the False Prophet.

Don't worry if this is unclear to you at the moment. I honestly believe all of this will become crystal clear as you get further in this book.

Now we must understand who or what each component of Satan's trinity represents. Let's begin with the Dragon:

The Dragon

Who or what is the Dragon? The Bible is clear on this. Revelation 12:9 says,

> "And the great dragon was cast out, that old serpent, called the Devil, and Satan, which deceiveth the whole world: he was cast out into the earth, and his angels were cast out with him."

So, the Dragon is another name for Satan or the Devil. John confirms this idea a few chapters later by substituting the Devil's name in place of the Dragon. Revelation 20:10 says,

> "And the **devil** that deceived them was cast into the lake of fire and brimstone, where the **beast** and the **false prophet** are, and shall be tormented day and night for ever and ever."

It's simple; the Dragon is Satan.

With that understanding, let me turn your attention back to Revelation 12 as we see this Dragon operating through a particular nation. The chapter provides insight into what nation it was.

> "And his tail drew the third part of the stars of heaven, and did cast them to the earth: and the dragon stood before the woman which was ready to be delivered, for to devour her child as soon as it was born." Revelation 12:4

Please understand that the Book of Revelation is not written in chronological order. It goes backward, forward, and sometimes sideways. Here, it appears that John the Revelator wants us to know that the power he is introducing as the Dragon is the same being that made war against Jesus in heaven; and that same being that made war against Jesus in heaven was the same being that was making war against Jesus on earth.

It is also important to note that during the earthly war on Christ, Satan operated under the guise of Imperial Rome.

According to Matthew 2:1-16, Satan used the Roman-appointed King Herod in an attempt to destroy

Christ. This was the kingdom of Rome, but not Christian Rome; this was Pagan Rome. Therefore, we must understand that the Dragon not only represents Satan, but it also represents Pagan Rome. Ellen White's commentary agrees with this view:

> "The chief agent of Satan in making war upon Christ and his people during the first centuries of the Christian era was the Roman Empire, in which paganism was the prevailing religion. Thus, while the dragon, primarily, represents Satan, it is, in a secondary sense, a symbol of pagan Rome."[15]

Likewise, we must realize that the Dragon not only represents Pagan Rome, but all of Paganism's enterprises, such as Mysticism, Spiritualism, Heathenism, Witchcraft, and their distant cousin, Astrology. There are times we should interpret the Dragon in its purest sense, which is Satan, and there are other times we should interpret "the Dragon" as a symbol for Pagan Rome or one of Satan's enterprises. Context is the key.

Revelation 12's interpretation of the Dragon appears to transition back and forth between the pure meaning of the word and the umbrella meaning of the word. Sometimes the Dragon represents Satan, and other times it represents an enterprise synonymous with Satan. In Revelation 12, Pagan Rome is the primary enterprise that stands under the umbrella of the Dragon.

---

[15] Ellen White, The Great Controversy 1888 p. 438

Now, what you may have missed is that Rome was not the first kingdom linked to the Dragon. Before Rome, there was another. Notice who was called a Dragon long before Rome:

> "Speak, and say, Thus saith the Lord GOD; Behold, I am against thee, Pharaoh king of Egypt, the great **dragon**..." Ezekiel 29:3

Egypt was known as the Dragon long before Rome. Comparing the Roman Empire to the Egyptian Empire allows us to see their similarities. Understand, the Dragon power has always wanted to exterminate the people of God. The Dragon's tactics against God's people in Egypt were almost identical to his tactics against God's people in Rome. Looking at the information that you are about to see, it should be clear to you that Satan's tactics against God's people have not changed.

Notice how the Dragon of Rome followed the Dragon of Egypt's example:

God's people in Egypt and Rome	The Dragon in Egypt	The Dragon in Rome
Both experienced an attempt by the Dragon to destroy all male babies born	And Pharaoh charged all his people, saying, **Every son that is born ye shall cast into the river**... Exodus 1:22	...and the dragon stood before the woman which was ready to be delivered, for to **devour her child as soon as it was born**. Revelation 12:4
Both had to flee into the wilderness as a result of the	...The LORD God of the Hebrews hath sent me unto thee, saying, Let my people go, that they may	And the woman fled into the **wilderness**, where she hath a place prepared of God... Revelation 12:6

Dragon's persecution	serve me in the **wilderness**... Exodus 7:16	
Both were helped with eagle's wings	...**I bare you on eagles' wings**, and brought you unto myself. Exodus 19:4	And to the woman were **given two wings of a great eagle**... Revelation 12:14
Both were trapped by water	But the Egyptians pursued after them...and overtook them encamping by **the sea**... Exodus 14:9	And the serpent cast out of his mouth **water as a flood** after the woman, that he might cause her to be carried away of the flood. Revelation 12:15
Both were saved on dry land	But **the children of Israel walked upon dry land** in the midst of the sea... Exodus 14:29	And **the earth helped the woman**... and swallowed up the flood... Revelation 12:16

I am merely driving home the point that Satan, the Dragon, has always desired to destroy God's people and has manifested himself through various heathen nations and entities to do it.

Now, let's deal with the second entity of the Devil's trinity—the Beast.

The Beast

Regarding the second entity of the Devil's trinity, John the Revelator says,

> "And I stood upon the sand of the sea, and saw a beast rise up out of the sea, having seven heads and ten horns, and upon his horns ten crowns, and upon his heads the name of blasphemy." Revelation 13:1.

Let's unpack this verse to avoid misinterpreting the message God is giving us through John the Revelator.

We've already established that a beast represents a kingdom. Thus, when John says he saw a beast in vision, he witnessed the rise of a world power. The sea is an important factor because Revelation 17:15 tells us, *"The waters which thou sawest...are peoples, and multitudes, and nations, and tongues."*

So, John witnessed the rising up of a nation in a region of the world where a concentration of various peoples, multitudes, nations, and tongues was prevalent. Simply put, it rose up in a heavily populated area of the world.

Then John says this nation had seven heads and ten horns and ten crowns upon his horns. Did you catch that? Revelation 13:1 says the Beast had ten horns with ten crowns, but back in Revelation 12:3, John said the Dragon had ten horns, but the horns were crownless!

It should be understood that when Pagan Rome dominated the world, the ten kings were crownless because they were part of the Roman Empire. Notice how Revelation 17:12 describes these crownless kings:

> "And the ten horns which thou sawest are ten kings, which have received no kingdom as yet; but receive power as kings one hour with the beast."

Let me ask you a question: If a king has no kingdom, should he be wearing a crown? Please understand that the ten horns in Revelation 12 are synonymous with the ten kings of Revelation 17. In Revelation 17, these kings had no kingdom, and in

Revelation 12, they had no crowns. Both represent the Roman Empire *before* it began crumbling into the smaller nations of Europe and the Middle East.

However, in the last days, the Roman Empire returns, but this time it returns as a union of independent nations to help restore the Papacy and create a worldwide union. In essence, these ten horns return in the last days with ten crowns. Understand that the crowns help us determine which phase of Rome is being highlighted. The crownless horns on the Dragon symbolize the Pagan Roman dispensation, and the crowned horns on the Beast symbolize the Papal Roman dispensation.

Ladies and Gentlemen, as the Roman Empire began crumbling, the Bishop of Rome became more powerful and began to acquire imperial-like powers in addition to religious authority. This was the beginning of what would be known as the Papacy[16], which is symbolized as a Beast in Revelation 13:1-3.

Notice the three animal components that make up Papal Rome:

> "And the beast which I saw was like unto a **leopard**, and his feet were as the feet of a **bear**, and his mouth as the mouth of a **lion**: and the dragon gave him his power..." Revelation 13:2

Have you seen these three beasts before? Of course you have! Notice what Daniel saw in vision:

> "And four great beasts came up from the sea, diverse one from another. The first

---

[16] Philip Van Ness Myers, A History of Rome p. 236

was like a **lion**...And behold another beast, a second, like to a **bear**...After this I beheld, and lo another, like a **leopard**...After this I saw in the night visions, and behold a fourth beast, dreadful and terrible, and strong exceedingly; and it had great iron teeth: it devoured and brake in pieces, and stamped the residue with the feet of it: and it was diverse from all the beasts that were before it; and it had ten horns."
Daniel 7:3-7

Did you catch that? Daniel saw a lion, a bear, a leopard, and then a terrible Beast. John saw a terrible Beast, with characteristics of a leopard, a bear, and a lion.

Notice that the order of Daniel's list is the exact opposite of John's list. Understand, the reason for this inversion is that Daniel was living during the time of the lion, and his vision was forward-looking to the terrible Beast, which was Rome. John, on the other hand, lived during the time of the terrible Beast (Rome), but his vision looked back to the kingdoms that came prior to Rome.

Now, an honest question is—How did the Papacy obtain its power? The answer is given:

"...and the dragon gave him his power, and his seat, and great authority."
Revelation 13:2

So here we see a transition taking place. The same power, the same seat, and the same authority that Pagan

Rome had was given to the Beast—Papal Rome. Ellen White provides additional commentary on this point with the following statement:

> "In the sixth century the papacy had become firmly established. Its seat of power was fixed in the imperial city, and the bishop of Rome was declared to be the head over the entire church. Paganism had given place to the papacy. The dragon had given to the beast "his power, and his seat, and great authority."[17]

Papal Rome would rule for roughly 1260 years, which is confirmed by Revelation 13:5:

> "And there was given unto him a mouth speaking great things and blasphemies; and power was given unto him to continue forty and two months."

The 42-month timeframe began in 538 AD with the establishment of the Papacy and ended in 1798 AD when Pope Pius VI was captured and taken prisoner.[18] This historical event is noted in the following scripture:

> "And I saw one of his heads as it were wounded to death; and his deadly wound was healed: and all the world wondered after the beast." Revelation 13:3

---

[17] Ellen White, The Great Controversy p. 54
[18] Ellen White, The Great Controversy p. 266

Remembering that a man isn't always a man in Bible prophecy helps us understand that this verse is not telling us that the Pope's literal head was wounded, but that the head of the system known as the Papacy is what received the deadly wound. Please also keep in mind that even though the Papacy received a fatal wound, that wound did not result in a fatality, for in the same verse, it tells us that "... *his deadly wound was healed: and all the world wondered after the beast."* This scripture makes it known that the Papacy will rise again; however, the Papacy's return to supremacy may not be what most are expecting. I will explain this a little later.

Now, we come to our final member of the Devil's trinity.

The False Prophet
Notice how John the Revelator describes this nation:

> "And I beheld another beast coming up out of the earth; and he had two horns like a lamb, and he spake as a dragon."
> Revelation 13:11

We already know that a beast is a nation, however, I want you to take note of the timeframe that this final Beast rose to power. This Beast with two horns showed up *after* the Pope was taken captive. This reveals to us that this final world power would rise to prominence not long after the decline of the Papacy in 1798 AD.

Next, John reveals that the region of the world that this power would rise from would be the earth. Remember what water represents? Revelation 17:15 tells us that water represents *peoples, and multitudes, and nations, and tongues.*

Now, if water represents a heavily populated area filled with multitudes of people, then the earth or land must describe the exact opposite—a sparsely populated region of the world.

John is telling us that this next world power would not rise in the heavily populated regions of the Old World; no, this nation would rise in the sparsely populated regions of the New World.

John didn't want us to have any doubt in our minds as to who this power was. Revelation 12, which is told from the Dragon's vantage point, makes a very interesting statement about water. It says,

> "And the serpent cast out of his mouth water as a flood after the woman, that he might cause her to be carried away of the flood." Revelation 12:15

Keep in mind that a flood is nothing more than water in destruction mode. In other words, this water that came after God's people in the form of a flood represented peoples, multitudes, and nations, and tongues in destruction mode. Another name for this destruction mode is called persecution.

For 1260 years, God's people were trying to survive the "floodwater," but then Revelation 12:16 says, *"And the earth helped the woman, and the earth opened her mouth and swallowed up the flood which the dragon cast out of his mouth."*

Wait a minute! Did you catch that?

Revelation 12:16 tells us that the earth helped the woman (God's people) from the persecution of Rome. Then Revelation 13:11 says a nation came up out of the earth following the fall of Papal Rome.

Don't miss this part!

The earth that helped the persecuted Christians in Revelation 12:16 is the same earth from which the lamb-like Beast in Revelation 13:11 ascended. Understanding this land is what helped persecuted Christians allows us to see that this particular nation helped give sanctuary to those who were being persecuted in the floodwaters of Europe.

Would you happen to know any nation that arose in a sparsely populated area of the world after the downfall of the Papacy, which became a place of sanctuary for those fleeing the persecutions of Europe?

John doesn't stop there; he gives us even *more* information on this final world power. He then reveals that "*he had two horns like a lamb.*" Now ask yourself this question: In Scripture, what does a lamb represent? We don't have to guess; John the Baptist answers that question for us:

> "The next day John seeth Jesus coming unto him, and saith, Behold the Lamb of God, which taketh away the sin of the world." John 1:29

The Bible is clear that a lamb represents Christ. Revelation 13 describes a Beast with horns resembling those of a lamb, indicating that the kingdom in question presents itself as a Christian nation.

Now, let's lay out all of our evidence to see which kingdom is being spoken of in Revelation 13:

- We have a nation that rose to prominence after the fall of the Papacy in 1798 AD.
- We have a nation that rose to prominence in a sparsely populated area of the world.
- We have a nation that gave sanctuary to Christians fleeing the persecutions of Europe.
- We have a nation that appears to be Christian in its principles.

The Bible is clear. The False Prophet is none other than the United States of America!

- The United States of America signed its Declaration of Independence in 1776 AD; however, it didn't officially rise to world power status until 1898 AD,[19] which was exactly 100 years after the fall of the Papacy. The US maintains its world power status to this day.

- The United States of America did not rise in the heavily populated Old European World; it rose in the sparsely populated New World of the Americas.

---

[19] Lukacs, John. A Thread of Years. United Kingdom: Yale University Press, 1999 pg. 127

- The United States of America was a region of the world where many Pilgrims and Puritans fled to escape the persecutions of Europe.

- The United States has presented itself as a Christian nation. Even though some are currently challenging this view, the United States is still considered a Christian country.

So now we should have a clear idea of who the False Prophet is. The False Prophet is the United States of America!

Now the question is—Why is the lamb-like Beast called the False Prophet? This is not difficult to understand once we know the role of a prophet. The Book of Jeremiah tells us what a prophet's role is:

> "Then the LORD put forth his hand, and touched my mouth. And the LORD said unto me, Behold, I have put my words in thy mouth." Jeremiah 1:9

Simply put, a prophet is like God's mouthpiece. He or she delivers messages directly from the Lord. However, this prophet in Revelation 13 is called a False Prophet—hence it speaks with the voice of the Dragon.

John confirms this in verse 11 when he says, "...*and he spake as a dragon.*" The False Prophet appeared to be Christian, but his words were those of Satan, the Dragon. The natural follow-up question to this is—What does a Dragon sound like? The answer to this is found in Revelation 12:10 when it says, "...*the accuser of our brethren is cast down, which accused them before our God day and night.*" Here, we can see that when the Dragon speaks, it's a voice of accusation.

When America begins speaking with the voice of the Dragon, it will begin to accuse innocent people of breaking the law. Through legislation, we will see the nation once known for its freedom become very intolerant. It may seem impossible, but the Bible is telling us that in the near future, the United States will make laws and declarations that will fulfill the Dragon's plan. I cannot say it more plainly than this: One day, the United States of America will enact laws that will be oppressive towards anyone who decides to follow God according to the Bible.

This Beast also makes fire come from heaven, revives the image of the Beast, and causes others to worship the first Beast. In essence, it counterfeits many of the functions that Biblical prophets have performed. However, we must remember that we are not dealing with a prophet of God; we are dealing with a prophet of Satan.

Please understand that this book's message is not anti-American. However, I cannot hide the fact that prophecy declares what this nation will do in the future.

The United States will establish Great Babylon

What you should also notice is that the second half of Revelation 13 is the only place we see the Dragon, Beast, and False Prophet working together before probation closes:

"And I beheld **another beast** coming up out of the earth; and he had two horns like a lamb, and he spake as a **dragon**. And he exerciseth all the power of the **first beast** before him..." Revelation 13:11-12

What you should now see is that the three-fold union of Dragon, Beast, and False Prophet is established under the auspices of the United States of America. This is an important point, as you will soon see that the United States of America is the nation that will utilize the powers of its predecessors to bring about the Time of Trouble.

Remember, the Dragon, the Beast, and the False Prophet are a trinity; they are three, but they are really one. How do I know this? Remember, earlier we read Revelation 16:13, which said, *"And I saw three unclean spirits like frogs come out of the mouth of the dragon, and out of the mouth of the beast, and out of the mouth of the false prophet."* Well, this is a three-fold union that appears later on in the same chapter, but notice the details provided about this union:

> "And the great city was divided into **three parts**, and the cities of the nations fell: and **great Babylon** came in remembrance before God, to give unto her the cup of the wine of the fierceness of his wrath." Revelation 16:19

Ellen White and the Three-fold Union

The Dragon, the Beast, and the False Prophet are the three components of Great Babylon! Notice how Ellen White presents them in her commentary:

> "The **Protestants of the United States** will be foremost in stretching their hands across the gulf to grasp the hand of **Spiritualism**; they will reach over the abyss to clasp hands with the **Roman power**; and under the influence of this <u>**THREEFOLD UNION**</u>, this country will follow in the steps of Rome in trampling on the rights of conscience."[20]

Can you spot the three components of Babylon in the above quotation? Their descriptions may be slightly different, but they are the same characters.

- Spiritualism is another name for the Dragon
- The Roman Power is another name for the Beast
- The Protestants of the United States is another name for the False Prophet

Here's another quote:

> "The sins of <u>**BABYLON**</u> will be laid open. The fearful results of a **union of Church and State**, the inroads of **Spiritualism**,

---

[20] Ellen White, The Great Controversy p. 588

the stealthy but rapid progress of **the papal power**,—all will be unmasked."[21]

In the above quote, Spiritualism represents the Dragon, the Papal power represents the Beast, and the union of Church and State represents the False Prophet. The sins of Babylon represent the activities of Satan's trinity!

Ellen White refers to these three powers once again:

"The **papal power**, the man of sin which thought to change times and laws, that had presented a rival sabbath to the world to be worshiped, the apostate power who sits in the temple of God showing himself that he is God, the power that drank the blood of the saints is united with **the Protestant churches**, having two horns like a lamb but speaks as a dragon; the deceptions of **spiritualism** which have perpetuated Satan's lie uttered in Eden, "Thou shalt not surely die" [Genesis 3:4]—all these are bound up in bundles, a corrupt harmony under a corrupt leader."[22]

Once you become familiar with the components of Babylon, you will be able to spot this trinity throughout Ellen White's writings.

So there we have it! The Devil's trinity is the Dragon, the Beast, and the False Prophet. They are three, but in reality, they are one.

---

[21] Ellen White, The Spirit of Prophecy Vol4 p. 424
[22] Ellen White, Manuscript 16, 1884

It is also important to understand that Satan tries to counterfeit almost everything God does. Would it surprise you to know that Satan's trinity attempts to counterfeit the Godhead?

Notice the stark similarities:

- God established his belief system called Judaism.
- The Dragon established his belief system called Paganism.

- God, in order to save mankind, sent His Son. (John 3:16)
- The Dragon, in order to destroy mankind, sent the Beast. (Revelation 13:1)

- Jesus' ministry lasted for three and a half years.
- The Beast's ministry of persecution lasted for three and a half prophetic years. (Revelation 13:5)

- Jesus was crucified at the end of His ministry. (Matthew 27:35)
- The Beast received a deadly wound at the end of its ministry. (Revelation 13:3)

- Jesus was resurrected from the dead. (Mark 16:9)
- The Beast's deadly wound was healed. (Revelation 13:3)

- The Holy Spirit was sent to testify of Christ. (John 15:26)
- The False Prophet arrives and makes an image to the Beast. (Revelation 13:14)

- The Holy Spirit used cloven tongues of fire in order to bring men into the truth. (Acts 2:3)
- The False Prophet brings fire down from heaven to deceive mankind. (Revelation 13:13)

- The Holy Spirit brings the seal of God. (Ephesians 1:13)
- The False Prophet causes all to receive the Mark of the Beast (Revelation 13:16)

I want to be crystal clear. You may not believe in the Trinity, but the Devil does. His trinity is what makes up Great Babylon. They are three, but they operate as one.

We are almost there. One last point needs to be made.

Rule 3: **Revelation 17 sheds additional light on Revelation 13.**

Now, I can understand how this particular point comes across as almost oxymoronic. How can you further reveal a Revelation? Let me show you. Notice what Revelation says about the Beast with seven heads and ten horns:

"And the angel said unto me, Wherefore didst thou marvel? I will tell thee the mystery of the woman, and of the beast that carrieth her, which hath the seven heads and ten horns." Revelation 17:7

Question: When did John first see the Beast with seven heads and ten horns? Answer: The first time John saw the seven-headed Beast was in Revelation 13, but Revelation 17 is where the angel revealed the mystery of the Beast. In other words, Revelation 17 sheds additional light on what John saw in Revelation 13.

Think about it! How did we come to know that the water from which the Beast emerged represented a heavily populated region? It is because Revelation 17:15 revealed that the water represents peoples, multitudes, nations, and tongues.

Again, how did we discover that the ten horns with crowns represented the ten kings in the last days? It is because Revelation 17:12 revealed to us that during the time of John, those kings had not yet received their kingdoms.

Don't you see it? Revelation 17 provides further details on some of the characteristics of the Beast that were seen in Revelation 13. This point may seem insignificant now, but I'm about to show you why this is the most crucial point out of all three.

Restating the Three Rules

Now, let's use these three rules to serve as our guide to understanding the meaning of 666. Let's remember what they are:

1. A man in Bible prophecy can refer to a kingdom, nation, or political system.
2. Satan's kingdom consists of three parts that work together as one, which is also known as Great Babylon.
3. If you are unclear about symbolism in Revelation 13, check to see if it's explained in Revelation 17.

I know we took the long scenic route to get here, but you are finally ready to grasp The True Meaning of 666!

I feel like a Karate instructor who has been teaching his students through trivial exercises, like applying wax to a car. As my students, I know you have been feverishly waxing the car for a while, and some of you have become weary of the task. However, as your Karate instructor, I am about to reveal that the waxing motion you have been doing is the foundation of being a Karate expert! So, as your "instructor," I'm here to tell you—You are ready, young Grasshopper!

Whether you realize it or not, you now have all the tools to understand the Biblical meaning of 666; you just haven't realized it yet. Spiritually, all the pieces of the puzzle have been handed to you, but you just need someone to rearrange a few of those pieces, and then you will see the beautiful work of art that you have at your mind's fingertips. You are about to understand the Biblical meaning of 666.

Chapter 4

The Biblical Meaning of 666

I want you to know that the Bible tells us the EXACT meaning of 666. All we need to do is piece the information together that the Bible provides us, and everything should become clear.

First, let's go back to where it all began. Let's review Revelation 13:18 one more time:

> "Here is wisdom. Let him that hath understanding count the number of the beast: for it is the number of a man; and his number is Six hundred threescore and six."

Look closely at this text. For the majority of my life, I made a fundamental mistake when reading this text. And if you are like me, you are probably making the same mistake. When I read this scripture, I placed my whole focus on looking for something in the Word of God that contained the number 666 in it. I now know this was a mistake. My emphasis was on the wrong component of this verse. Trying to find some other reference in the Bible that contains 666 is a logical approach, but in this instance, the wrong approach. I only know this now because God revealed it to me.

When I couldn't find a key reference to 666 from

other Scriptures, I focused on the word "man" in the text. However, as you already know, this was also an incorrect approach to understanding the mystery of 666.

This whole time, my focus, when reading Revelation 13:18, overlooked the one component of this scripture that gives us insight into what 666 really means. Understand, we cannot decipher the meaning of 666 by searching for the number 666 or looking for a distinguished man. I'm here to tell you that the most important part of Revelation 13:18 is the part we have always overlooked. The part that says, "*Here is wisdom.*"

Here is Wisdom

You see, this one simple phrase makes writing this whole book possible. It might sound crazy, but without this one phrase, we may have never received an understanding of 666. "*Here is Wisdom*" tells us exactly what 666 means!

Now I'm going to show you why this phrase is the key to unlocking the meaning of 666. It is now time for me to show you just how beneficial your "waxing-on" and "waxing-off" have become. Let's begin by utilizing one of the three rules we developed earlier.

Remember rule number three? In case you forgot, this rule says, "If you are unclear about symbolism in Revelation 13, check to see if it's explained in Revelation 17." Now, let's use some critical thinking. Turn to Revelation 17 and tell me if you can find any scripture that has a phrase similar to the "*Here is wisdom*" phrase found in Revelation 13:18. Don't worry; I can wait.

Alright, times up.

You should have discovered that the beginning of Revelation 17:9 is similar to the beginning of Revelation 13:18. This is not a coincidence!

> Revelation 13:8 says, "Here is **wisdom**."
> Revelation 17:9 says, "Here is the mind which hath **wisdom**."

It's almost a direct quote!!

The transliteration of the word "wisdom" in the original Greek is *Sophia*. The transliteration of the words "mind" and "understanding" in the original Greek is *Nous*.

Now, look at the construction of Revelation 13:18 and Revelation 17:9 and tell me if you can see the obvious connection between these two verses:

> Revelation 13:18 says, "Here is *Sophia*. Let him that hath *Nous* count the number of the beast..."

> Revelation 17:9 says - "And here is the *Nous* which hath *Sophia*..."

It's as if Revelation 13:18 is saying – Here is the wisdom of he who has the mind, and Revelation 17:9 is saying – Here is the mind of he who has wisdom. These two verses almost come together like a yin and yang scenario.

Now that we have established an obvious link between Revelation 13:18 and Revelation 17:9, I think it's probably in our best interest to find out what the rest of 17:9 says, don't you?

The Seven Mountains

Notice Revelation 17:9 in its fullness:

> "And here is the mind which hath wisdom. The seven heads are seven mountains, on which the woman sitteth."

Remember, I told you that we would come back to these seven heads! And now you will see why I saved the seven heads until the end.

The Bible clearly says that these seven heads are seven mountains on which the woman (false religion) sits. The obvious question is— If the seven heads are also seven mountains, then what are the mountains? Don't miss a word of what I'm about to tell you because the Bible reveals to us precisely what these mountains are:

> "And I will render unto Babylon and to all the inhabitants of Chaldea all their evil that they have done in Zion in your sight, saith the LORD. Behold, I am against thee, O destroying **mountain**, saith the LORD, which destroyest all the earth: and I will stretch out mine hand upon thee, and roll thee down from the rocks, and will make thee a burnt mountain." Jeremiah 51:24-25

Did you catch that? God called literal Babylon a destroying mountain. This helps us understand that a mountain in Bible prophecy can represent a political government or kingdom!!

So, a head represents a mountain, which also represents a kingdom! And in case you are still not convinced, the very next verse in Revelation 17 confirms that these seven heads are, in fact, seven kingdoms. Notice what Revelation 17:10 says:

> "And there are seven kings..."

Don't forget, God often refers to a kingdom by its king. And just in case you are tempted to believe these kings are flesh and blood men, remember rule number one: A man in Bible prophecy sometimes refers to a kingdom, nation, or political system. (Wax-on, young Grasshopper!)

I'm merely setting the precedent that these seven heads are also seven mountains, which are also seven governments. They all refer to the same seven entities.

Now, the logical question here is— What are these seven heads? Well, for starters, the Bible already identifies one of these heads for us. Do you remember? If you've forgotten, then turn to Revelation 13:3, which says, "*And I saw* **one of his heads** *as it were wounded to death; and his deadly wound was healed: and all the world wondered after the beast.*"

Are you seeing this? John, in Revelation 13, reveals to us that one of the heads received a deadly wound. We previously established that the head who received this wound was the Papacy! So, we know what one of those heads represents. Now we just need to understand who the other six heads signify.

Pay close attention! Notice the clue Revelation

17:9 tells us about these other kingdoms:

> "And there are seven kings: five are fallen..."

Hold it right there! Think about what you are reading. There are seven kings; however, five of those kings have already fallen. If five have fallen, then what is the number of the current king?

Let me help you visualize this. Here are the seven kings:

But remember, the Bible told us that five of them had already fallen. So, if five out of the seven kings had already fallen, we can clearly see that the current king, at that time, was the sixth king, right?

This means that when John wrote this statement, it was during the time of the sixth king. Do you see it yet? Think about what I just told you:

- Revelation 13:18 talks about **wisdom** and then mentions the number **666**.
- Revelation 17:9-10 talks about **wisdom** and then refers to the **6th** king!!!

Both scriptures contain the word "wisdom," and

both scriptures refer to the number six! This is not a coincidence!

But we can't dwell here. We must move on. Now we need to understand what nation represents the sixth king. Revelation 17:10 says,

> "And there are seven kings: five are fallen, and one is..."

We can determine who the sixth king was by asking the simple question: What kingdom ruled the world when John wrote The Revelation? The answer is Rome. However, we must be more specific. Just saying "Rome" is not enough. We must establish which phase of Rome was ruling at this time. And I believe there is no debate that John lived during the reign of Pagan Rome.

So now we know that the sixth king was Pagan Rome. We also know that the seventh king was Papal Rome. Now we must decipher the identity of the five kings who had already fallen. Let's point them out, beginning with the fifth king:

- Greece ruled the known world before its divided territory was conquered by Pagan Rome. Greece was the fifth kingdom.
- Persia ruled the known world before Greece conquered it. Persia was the fourth kingdom.[23]

---

[23] Initially, Media co-ruled with Persia (Daniel 5:28). However, the Medes were eventually subdued by the Persians (Daniel 8:3), which is why Persia is listed as the fourth world power as opposed to Media-Persia.

- Babylon ruled the known world before Persia conquered it. Babylon was the third kingdom.
- Assyria ruled the known world before Babylon conquered it. Assyria was the second kingdom.
- Egypt ruled the known world before Assyria conquered it. Egypt was the first kingdom.

Here is an illustrated list of all seven kings in their proper numerical order:

1	2	3	4	5	6	7
Egypt	Assyria	Babylon	Persia	Greece	Pagan Rome	Papal Rome

Now, I can all but guarantee that someone who is well acquainted with Bible prophecy is wondering why I listed Egypt as the first kingdom when Daniel's vision began with Babylon.[24] The answer is very simple: Daniel lived during the time of Babylon; therefore, the visions he received would naturally begin with the power that was ruling at that time. The Book of Revelation follows this same theme, which is why John's vision begins with Pagan Rome instead of Babylon.

The seven kingdoms provide us with the full scope of Satan's master plan. This is done by looking at the history of these various kingdoms that he's worked

---

[24] Egypt and Assyria are brought into Daniel's vision through the ribs in the Bear's mouth (Daniel 7:5).

through to complete that master plan. Now that we know who these seven kingdoms are, I want you to understand the criteria that were used to determine these kingdoms over other various peoples, multitudes, nations, and tongues:

- Each of these kingdoms was a world power at one time or another.
- Each of these kingdoms' territories encompassed where God's people dwelt.
- Each of these kingdoms persecuted God's people in one way or another.

This last point is crucial because it will be the basis for another statement that I will make at the end of this book.

The Beast that Was, Is Not, Yet Is

> "And there are seven kings: five are fallen, and one is, and the other is not yet come..." Revelation 17:10

If John the Revelator lived during the sixth king, and that's the one who "is," then who was the other that had "not yet come?"

You see, John the Revelator was telling us that five world powers had already fallen, and he was living during the time of the sixth world power—Pagan Rome. He also understood that another world power would come after Pagan Rome, but he didn't know who it would be or when it would appear; he only knew it was coming. What was considered John's future back then is considered today's history now. We now understand that the nation that rose to supremacy after Pagan Rome was Papal Rome. This kingdom was the *other* that had *not yet come.*

A Short Space

Assigning Papal Rome as the king who had *not yet come* puts us in a slightly precarious situation. The reason we find ourselves in this situation is that the end of Revelation 17:10 says, "*...and when he cometh, he must continue a short space.*"

Students of prophetic history know that Papal Rome's reign lasted 1260 years! Clearly, this was not a short period by any stretch. So, how do we explain the Papacy's 1260-year reign as a *short time*? This will take some following, so I hope you've had a good night's sleep and a well-balanced breakfast. I want you to understand that the "short time" of Revelation 17:10 is not actually a period *of* time but rather a period *in* time. Let me explain it like this: Remember, Revelation 12 shows us Satan's agenda from the Dragon's perspective. Look closely at vs. 12.

> "Therefore rejoice, ye heavens, and ye that dwell in them. Woe to the inhabiters of the earth and of the sea! for the devil is come down unto you, having great wrath, because he knoweth that he hath but a **short time**."

Did you see that? The Devil realized that he had a short time. Now, notice what happened right after this short time began:

THE BIBLICAL MEANING OF 666 • 75

"And when the dragon saw that he was cast unto the earth, he persecuted the woman which brought forth the man child. And to the woman were given two wings of a great eagle, that she might fly into the wilderness, into her place, where she is nourished for a time, and times, and half a time, from the face of the serpent." Revelation 12:13-14.

The time, times, and half a time represents the 1260 years of Papal rule. However, this rule only began after Satan realized that he had a short time. The *short time* of Revelation 12 and the *short space* of Revelation 17 both refer to the time in history that took place after Satan's big epiphany, which resulted in apostasy and then Papal persecution. Thus, the short space that is mentioned here in Revelation 17 does

> **A Time, Times, and Half a Time**
>
> According to Daniel 4:16, King Nebuchadnezzar was humbled for 7 times. Most Bible scholars agree this was a seven-year time span.
>
> So, Biblically speaking, a "time" refers to a year.
>
> Revelation 12:14 says that the woman was persecuted for a time, times, and half a time.
>
> Jewish calendar years consisted of 360 days.
>
> With that in mind:
>
> A time = 360 days
> Times = 720 days
> Half a time = 180 days
> ---------------------
>   1260 days
>
> In prophecy, it is often the case that a day equals a year. (see Numbers 14:34 and Ezekiel 4:6). Therefore, we conclude that this time period was 1260 years.

not refer to a duration of years as much as it establishes a period in history—the period that began with the apostasy of the Christian Church to the emergence of the Man of Sin. Satan's *short time* became evident in the Middle Ages but continues until Jesus returns as the true King of this world.

In this manner, we can confidently say that the Papacy is the power that "accompanies" Satan during his Short Time. Thus, the Papacy continues for a Short Space.

The Eighth King

Now that we have established the identity of the seven kings, I am going to show you something that is going to flip everything on its head. Hold on to your seats and watch this:

> "And the beast that was, and is not, even he is the **eighth**, and is of the seven, and goeth into perdition." Revelation 17:11

Wait a minute! John spent this whole time telling us that there were seven kingdoms, but now he mentions an eighth kingdom. Let me ask you a question—Who do you think the eighth kingdom could be? Many believe this is the return of the Papacy. However, the only way to interject the Papacy as the eighth king would be to ignore the current world power—the United States of America. Now, let's pause for a moment because I know someone reading this book right now is asking the question— If the eighth kingdom is the United States of America, then why do Daniel's prophecies all end with Papal Rome? In other words, if the USA is part of this list of seven heads, and if it is numbered with the seven world powers that are aiming to destroy God's people, shouldn't we be able to find some trace of this power in the book of Daniel? My answer to you is—The United States of America *is* in the Book of Daniel, but you may not have realized it. The reason many have not realized America is in the Book of Daniel is because most do not realize that the eighth kingdom is part of the seventh kingdom. Remember what John says about the last two world powers:

> "...he is the eighth, and is of the seven..."
> Revelation 17:11

According to John, the eighth is part of the seventh.[25] This reveals to us that, prophetically, America is the continuation of Papal Rome! Now we see those feet of iron and clay from Daniel 2 in a whole new light, don't we?

If you are reading Ellen White's writings, you should also know that Ellen White placed the United States of America as the final world power in prophecy:

> "At the time when the Papacy, robbed of its strength, was forced to desist from persecution, John beheld a new power coming up to echo the dragon's voice, and carry forward the same cruel and blasphemous work. This power, <u>the last that is to wage war against the church and the law of God, is represented by a beast with lamblike horns</u>."[26]

---

[25] Hepta in the Greek can mean seven or seventh. See G2033 - hepta - Strong's Greek Lexicon (KJV). Retrieved from
https://www.blueletterbible.org//lang/lexicon/lexicon.cfm?Strongs=G2033&t=KJV
[26] Ellen White, Signs of the Times February 8, 1910

Notice Ellen White says that the United States is the last power to wage war. While this statement contradicts our traditional eschatological viewpoint, it also confirms that the eighth head CANNOT be the Papacy. It must be the United States of America.

The Number of the Beast

I believe the sixth, seventh, and eighth powers are also identified in Revelation 17:8. Notice how they are identified:

> "The beast that thou sawest was, and is not; and shall ascend out of the bottomless pit, and go into perdition: and they that dwell on the earth shall wonder, whose names were not written in the book of life from the foundation of the world, when they behold the beast that **WAS**, and **IS NOT**, and **YET IS**." Revelation 17:8

- Pagan Rome was the power that WAS (meaning it was already in existence)
- The Papacy was the power that IS NOT
- The United States is the power that YET IS

To some, this might sound a little confusing. It's as if John is saying that this power used to exist, but no longer exists, but in actuality still exists. Hopefully, this will become clear as we come to a crescendo. Let's review our final list of kingdoms:

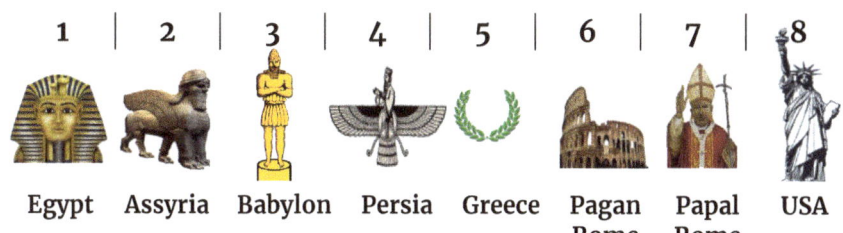

Remembering that five of these kingdoms had already fallen. Remembering that Pagan Rome is the Dragon, Papal Rome is the Beast, and the USA is the False Prophet, we now must do what John told us to do in Revelation 13:18. Do you remember? Let me remind you.

> "Let him that hath understanding count the number of the beast..." Revelation 13:18

What you may not realize is that the Beast's number in Revelation 13 that we are to count is not just the Papacy. This Beast is False Protestantism of the United States, Paganism of Rome, and the Papacy combined. In other words, the Beast of Revelation 13:18 is the threefold union known as Great Babylon. Now the question we must answer is—What is Great Babylon's number?

Great Babylon's Number

Whether you realize it or not, you now have the wisdom. All you need to do is simply count. We don't need geometry, we don't need trigonometry, we don't even need algebra, and we definitely don't need gematria. All we need to do is count. However, before we begin counting, let me remind you of rule number two. Do you remember what it says? Satan's kingdom consists of three parts that work together as one. Don't miss this! In other words, Pagan Rome, Papal Rome, and the United States of America all work together. They are prophetically the same kingdom!

Notice how The Great Controversy emphasizes this same fact:

> "<u>Both heathen and papists were actuated by the same dragon spirit</u>. They differed only in that the Romish apostate, making a pretense of serving God, was the more dangerous and cruel foe. Through the agency of Romanism., Satan took the world captive. The professed church of God was swept into the ranks of this delusion, and for more than a thousand years the true people of God suffered under the dragon's ire. At the time when the Papacy, robbed of its strength, was forced to desist from persecution, John beheld a new power coming up to <u>echo the dragon's voice</u>..."[27]

Ellen White saw that the Dragon was also present in the Papacy's Beast and the False Prophet's United States. Thus, she was able to make the proclamation that the two powers that succeeded Pagan Rome still had the "dragon spirit," or the "dragon's voice." The Bible

---

[27] Ellen White, Signs of the Times Feb 8, 1910.

further confirms this fact when we realize how Revelation 12 and 13 highlight the Dragon in all three powers. Notice what the Bible says in Revelation 12:3.

> "And there appeared another wonder in heaven; and behold a great red **DRAGON**..."

Then Revelation 13 highlights the Beast, but notice who gave the Beast his power, seat, and great authority:

> "And the beast which I saw was like unto a leopard, and his feet were as the feet of a bear, and his mouth as the mouth of a lion: and the **DRAGON** gave him his power, and his seat, and great authority." Revelation 13:2

Then Revelation 13:11 highlights the lamb-like Beast (aka the False Prophet), but notice how he speaks:

> "And I beheld another beast coming up out of the earth; and he had two horns like a lamb, and he spake as a **DRAGON**." Revelation 13:11

In essence, these three powers, known as the Dragon, the Beast, and the False Prophet, are in reality the DRAGON, the DRAGON, and the DRAGON! Now, if we count the kingdoms again, what number is assigned to the Dragon? The Dragon represents the sixth kingdom! So even though the literal, chronological order of the Dragon, Beast, and False Prophet is six, seven, and eight, spiritually, their chronological order is **SIX, SIX, SIX**!!!

Now it's clear! John the Revelator was trying to get us to understand that the Dragon is not dead. He continues to live through the seventh and eighth kingdoms. Now our eyes have been opened, and we see that the Bible views Pagan Rome, Papal Rome, and the United States of America as one and the same!

> The sixth kingdom is called the Dragon.
> The seventh kingdom is called the Beast.
> The eighth kingdom is called the False Prophet.
>
> The sixth kingdom "was."
> The seventh kingdom "is not."
> The eighth kingdom "yet is."
>
> The sixth kingdom is Pagan Rome.
> The seventh kingdom is Papal Rome.
> The eighth kingdom is Protestant Rome.
>
> The sixth kingdom is the Dragon.
> The seventh kingdom has the power, seat, and authority of the Dragon.
> The eighth kingdom has the voice of the Dragon.

Regardless of how society views these three kingdoms, God views them as the sixth kingdom, and again the sixth kingdom, and once again, the sixth kingdom! So, even though the last three world powers have been fundamentally different, in reality, they have been the same. The Devil's agenda was visible in Pagan Rome; his agenda was masked in Papal Rome; and one day, his agenda will be carried out by Protestant America.

Now Revelation 13:18 makes sense. John, after exposing the careers of the Dragon, the Beast, and the False Prophet, culminates everything that was revealed about these three powers in the very last verse of chapter 13. Now we understand why he labeled them 666.

John's message to the believers is simply this: One day, Pagan Rome will fall, but don't be deceived because Pagan Rome will manifest itself again as Papal Rome. However, one day Papal Rome will fall, but don't fall asleep because Papal Rome will return as the United States of America.

The Dragon, the Beast, and the False Prophet are like an old horror movie. When I was a little younger, I saw a film about a pet animal. This animal died and was buried. However, the animal came back to life again and haunted the family! Ladies and Gentlemen, Pagan Rome was dead and buried, but it came back to life as Papal Rome. Papal Rome received a deadly wound, but it showed up again as the United States of America. We are being haunted by the same Beast that was dead and buried! Now we understand, 666 is merely three different phases of the same power. This is an amazing message that God has given us.

Remember I told you earlier in this book that the Papacy will be revived, but not in the way you may think. Understand there is a Biblical principle that I was taught called *Repeat and Expand*. This principle teaches that prophecy often repeats itself, and when it repeats, it will provide additional information. We can see a first-hand example of this in the Book of Daniel. The image in Chapter 2 and the beasts of Chapter 7 refer to the same kingdoms. It repeats; however, chapter 7 provides more information regarding those kingdoms. In essence, the prophecy repeats and expands.

In Revelation 13, there is a repeat and expansion within the same chapter. Notice what vs. 3 says:

> "And I saw one of his heads as it were wounded to death and his deadly wound was healed: and all the world wondered after the beast."

We have already established that this wound was the downfall of the Papacy in 1798. This verse tells us that *his deadly wound was healed and all the world wondered after him*. However, if you read closely, you will discover that John repeats the prophecy regarding the Papacy. Notice what he says:

> "He that leadeth into captivity shall go into captivity: he that killeth with the sword must be killed with the sword. Here is the patience and the faith of the saints." Revelation 13:10

The wound in verse 3 and the captivity and death in verse 10 both represent the same historical event—the downfall of the Papacy.

Verse 3, however, records the Papacy's resurgence with these words: "*his deadly wound was healed: and all the world wondered after the beast.* But, there is no mention of the Papacy's resurgence in verse 10...until you realize the resurgence occurs in verse 11!

We have witnessed a repeat and expansion, but this time it does not say that the wound was healed, and all the world wondered after the beast. The very next scripture tells us that John "...*beheld another beast coming up out of the earth.*"

In Revelation 13:3, we are told that the Papacy will rise again, and the world will wonder after it; however, we are not told how this occurs. Revelation 13:12 repeats and expands so that we can understand how the Papacy will achieve this. Notice what John says:

> "And he exerciseth all the power of the first beast before him, and causeth the earth and them which dwell therein to worship the first beast, whose deadly wound was healed."

The United States of America will push the Papacy's agenda and enact laws contrary to God's commandments, which will be a revival of the Papacy. However, if you are waiting for the Papacy to garner power as it did during the Dark Ages, please understand that the Bible does not teach that. The Bible says that the Papacy will dominate the world again, but this time it will be through the False Prophet. You don't have to wait for a New World Order; the lamb-like Beast *is* the New World Order!

Here is something to ponder: If the seven previous world powers all persecuted the Saints, then what do you think the eighth world power is going to do? No matter how much it may appear that freedom of religion will continue to reign in America, the Bible says this nation will make an image to Papal Rome. The same results that Satan brought about in the first seven kingdoms will be manifested once again in the eighth kingdom!

Ladies and Gentlemen, we must understand that Jesus is coming back again, but before he comes, the Dragon, the Beast, and the False Prophet will come against God's remnant believers. Knowing the meaning of 666 becomes irrelevant if we have not given our hearts to Jesus. Now is the time to decide if we want to see Jesus in peace or if we prefer to cry for the rocks to fall on us.

The Bible says, "*If you hear his voice, harden not your heart.*" (Hebrews 3:15). I pray that reading this important message has softened your heart towards God.

666 is now made up

Finally, I would be remiss if I did not revisit Ellen White's statement that I quoted at the beginning of this book. It deserves a little clarification. Let me remind you what she wrote in Word to the Little Flock:

> "...I saw that the number (666) of the Image Beast was made up."

God revealed to me that Ellen White was not suggesting that 666 was randomly made up. She was declaring that there was a sequence to 666 that had now been established. Let me explain it like this:

I have two young sons. One day, I told them they had to make up their beds before they could play with their toys.

After a few minutes, I heard them playing, so I asked them if they had made up their beds. Their response was, "Yes, Daddy."

I went upstairs to inspect. I opened their door and saw that both beds only had bottom sheets on them. The top sheets and covers were on the floor.

I went back downstairs and said to them, "Your beds are not yet made up. Please go back upstairs and make up your beds."

Not long afterward, I heard them playing once again. And I asked a second time if their beds were made up. They again replied, "Yes, Daddy."

So I went back upstairs and walked into their room. This time, the bottom sheet was still there, and now the top sheet was on the bed, but the covers were still on the floor.

I went back downstairs and firmly told them, "Your beds are still not made up. If I have to walk back up those stairs one more time and find those beds unmade, you will both be in big trouble."

After some time had passed, I witnessed the sound of children playing yet again. I calmly walked upstairs expecting the worst, but to my surprise, the bottom sheet was on, the top sheet was on, and the covers were there, and yes, their pillows were properly placed against the headboard. Finally, their beds were made up!

Now, Ellen White's statement makes sense. John the Revelator could not say 666 was made up in his day because he only lived during the first six. Martin Luther could not say 666 was made up because he only lived during the second six. Ellen White could make that declaration because, through the historical lens of prophecy, she saw the Dragon, she saw the Beast, and she lived during the False Prophet. And it was then, and only then, that she was able to declare that 666 was made up.

Ladies and Gentlemen, we no longer need to search for words that add up to 666. We no longer need to prove that Vicarius Filii Dei was on the Pope's tiara. No more attempts to justify using occult methods in order to determine Biblical truth. 666 is right there in the Word of God.

I finally found an explanation of 666 that I was comfortable believing. I was so excited to know that God *does* hear and answer our prayers! That Sunday morning, I rose from my knees with a little pep in my step! I resumed my Bible studies and dusted off some of Ellen White's books. I apologized to God, and I know for a fact that he has forgiven me.

And in case you are wondering, due to extenuating circumstances, I was never able to present this information to the church that I was preparing for, but that's how I came to the decision to write this book! Why only share this knowledge with a few hundred people when I can share it with the entire world?

And so there you have it; now you know my journey, now you know my story, and now you know The Clear and Present Truth of 666.

Chapter 5

Questions and Objections

You may have some questions or objections that were not answered in the earlier chapters of this book. Hopefully, I will be able to address them in this section.

Objection: In Revelation 13, the number is six hundred, sixty and six. Mathematically, this is not the same as 6.6.6.
Answer: This is correct. Numerically, the value of 666 is not the same as 6.6.6. (three individual sixes); however, what many may not have realized is that the Bible actually is not telling us to count the number of the Beast; it's telling us to calculate the number of the Beast. In verse 18, the word for "count," in the Greek, is psēphizō, which is better translated as "compute" or "calculate." Thus, even though the literal number is six hundred and sixty-six, we derive 666 from it as part of that calculation.

Question: How will Satan's 666 trinity be manifested in the last days?
Answer: 666 has a spiritual manifestation, but it also has a physical designation. The Dragon is Spiritualism, but its physical designation is the remnants of the Roman Empire—the European Union. The Beast is

Catholicism; its physical designation is the Vatican. Last but not least, the False Prophet is False Protestantism, which is located in the United States of America. These three powers will work together in the end of time to bring the nations into a New World Order. The Harlot will be the religion of the Order, and the worship of Satan will be its goal.

Question: The usage of Roman numerals is very common. Vicarius Filii Dei happens to be a group of Roman numerals that, added together, equals 666. How can you call this gematria?
Answer: To be clear, Vicarius Filii Dei is not a number; it's a phrase that many are deriving a number from. However, this is what gematria is at its core. Remember, the definition of Gematria is the practice of assigning numerical values to words based on the fixed numerical values of their letters. So, when we take a word and assign a numerical value in order to derive some form of knowledge based upon that number, that is gematria.

The usage of Roman numerals solely as numbers is acceptable, as this is not the same as deriving a system of truth from those numbers, as is being done with Vicarius Filii Dei. Thus, Roman numerals aren't inherently bad; it's how we use them that makes that determination.

Question: If the Mark of the Beast refers to the Papacy, how can the number of the Beast refer to Babylon?
Answer: Remember, the eighth kingdom is really part of the seventh; thus, we are dealing with different

phases of the same power. Therefore, the Mark (Sunday replacing the Sabbath) can only be attributed to the originator of the Papal phase, also called the Sea Beast. However, the number 666 must refer to the alliance phase of this power, and can only be attributed to the United States, which establishes the alliance by speaking like a Dragon and reviving the Sea Beast.

Question: How can Babylon be the number of a man when the Harlot in Revelation 17 had this same number on her forehead? Wouldn't this be the number of a woman?
Answer: In Revelation 17, we see a Harlot. According to verse 5, "...upon her forehead was a name written, MYSTERY, BABYLON THE GREAT..." In this manner, the Harlot represents Babylon. However, this is not at odds with the view taught in this book. Remember, the union of Church and State is symbolized by the union of a woman and a man. When a woman gets married, she often takes the man's name as part of her name. Here in Revelation 17, the Harlot is the religion of the threefold union and therefore takes on the name of her husband.

Objection: Ellen White's 666 reference in Word to the Little Flock didn't originally contain the number 666. This number was added by an outside source.
Answer: This is correct. When Ellen White wrote, "the number (666) of the Image Beast was made up," she did not write "666."[28] However, her usage of the phrase "the number," and the phrase "of the beast," in

---

[28] It is believed this was added by Joseph Bates

conjunction with her referring to the Mark of the Beast within the same paragraph, reveals that she was obviously referring to Revelation 13:18. Also, knowing that there's no other prophecy that refers to the number of a Beast, it's obvious she was referring to 666.

Objection: Ellen White endorsed Uriah Smith's book, which contained the Vicarius Filii Dei teaching. This means that Uriah Smith is correct.
Answer: Make no mistake—Ellen White was very fond of *Thoughts on Daniel and the Revelation*. Here's one of her most glowing statements in support of Smith's book:

> "The grand instruction contained in Daniel and Revelation has been eagerly perused by many in Australia. This book has been the means of bringing many precious souls to a knowledge of the truth. Everything that can be done should be done to circulate Thoughts on Daniel and the Revelation. I know of no other book that can take the place of this one. It is God's helping hand."[29]

While it's important to know what Ellen White said about Smith's book, it's equally important to recognize what Ellen White did not say. In other words, *Daniel and the Revelation* is an important book, but nowhere does she suggest that every viewpoint made in that book is correct. Those who view Smith's Daniel and the Revelation book in this manner are inadvertently viewing his book as an extension of Ellen White's

---

[29] Ellen White, Letters and Manuscripts — Volume 16 (1901)

inspiration. This was not the meaning behind Ellen White's glowing remarks about his book, nor should Adventists push this narrative in order to propagate their preferred views of Bible prophecy.

Those who place Smith's book on an inspiration pedestal should see that Smith's contemporaries did not see his book in this fashion. We know this to be true because when there was a controversy as to the meaning of the Daily, Ellen White made it clear what her position was:

> "I now ask that my ministering brethren shall not make use of my writings in their arguments regarding this question ["the daily"]; for I have had no instruction on the point under discussion, and I see no need for the controversy. Regarding this matter under present conditions, silence is eloquence."[30]

Although the subject of the Daily was covered by Uriah Smith, notice that the brethren did not refer to his writings for the meaning of the Daily. We should also notice that Ellen White did not refer them to Smith's book for its meaning either. This reveals that during the time of the pioneers, Smith's book had not yet been placed upon the inspiration pedestal that it is today. Therefore, I believe we should see Smith's Daniel and the Revelation for what it is—an amazing book on prophecy that is called God's helping hand, that should

---

[30] Ellen White, Selected Messages Book 1 p.164

continue to be circulated to bring many precious souls to the truth.

Objection: The Bible says it's the number of a man; that man is the Pope.

Answer: As Adventists, our theology doesn't rest upon one man. We recognize that the Antichrist represents a system. In the last days, the Man of Sin will not act alone; he will be in concert with the Dragon and the False Prophet. Therefore, we should understand that the "man" represents all three systems working as one power, thus, it is represented as one "man."

THE CLEAR AND PRESENT TRUTH OF
666

TEST YOUR KNOWLEDGE

1. True or False. The phrase Vicarius Filii Dei originated with the Seventh-day Adventist Church. (*p. 22*)

2. What is gematria? (*pp. 24-25*)

3. According to Daniel, a beast represents a _____ or a _____ (*p. 40*)

4. Who does Ellen White identify as the Man of Sin? (*p. 60*)

5. Who are the members of the Devil's trinity? (*p. 60*)

6. According to Revelation 12:9, who is the Dragon? (*p. 43*)

7. What nation was also called the Dragon in Revelation? (*p. 45*)

8. What else falls under the umbrella of the Dragon? (*p. 45*)

9. What does the sea represent in Bible prophecy? (*p. 48*)

10. What does the Beast in Revelation 13:1-3 represent? (*p. 49*)

11. Name the three animals that constituted the first Beast of Revelation 13. (*Revelation 13:2*)

12. Why does Daniel list these beasts in the opposite order that John the Revelator lists them? (*pp. 49-50*)

13. When did Papal dominance begin and end? (*p. 51*)

14. What nation represents the False Prophet? (*p. 55*)

15. List the attributes of the False Prophet that determine what nation it symbolizes. (*p. 55*)

16. What verse in the Bible declares the three in one aspect of the Dragon, the Beast, and the False Prophet? (*p. 58*)

TEST YOUR KNOWLEDGE ▪ 99

17. List the three rules used to determine the meaning of 666 (*p. 64*)

    _____
    _____
    _____
    _____

18. What phrase connects Revelation 13:18 to Revelation 17:9? (*pp. 66-67*)

    _____

19. What nations are represented by the seven kings? (*p. 72*)

    _____
    _____

20. Which of the seven heads received a deadly wound? (*p. 83*)

    _____

21. Explain how time, times, and half a time calculates to equal 1260 years? (*p. 75*)

    _____
    _____
    _____

22. Who is the eighth kingdom? (*p. 76*)

    _____
    _____

    Who gave the Beast his power, seat, and great authority? (*Revelation 13:2*)_____

    _____

23. Whose voice was given to the False Prophet? *(Revelation 13:11)*

_____

24. Explain the message of Revelation 13:18. *(p. 83)*

_____
_____

25. Explain in your own words what Ellen White meant when she said, "*I saw that the number (666) of the Image Beast was made up.*" *(pp. 86-87)*

_____
_____
_____
_____

26. The Dragon, Beast, and False Prophet are preparing their final stand against God's people. What changes need to be made in your life for you to be victorious?

_____
_____
_____
_____

ANSWERS

1. Vicarius Filii Dei originated with the Seventh-day Adventist Church. **False**.

2. What is gematria? **A numerological system used in kabbalah and other forms of Jewish mysticism that assigns numerical values to words based on the fixed numerical values of their letters**.

3. According to Daniel, a beast represents a **King** or a **Kingdom**.

4. Who does Ellen White identify as the Man of Sin? **The Papal power**

5. Who are the members of the Devil's trinity? **The Dragon, the Beast, and the False Prophet**

6. According to Revelation 12:9, who is the Dragon? **That old serpent called the Devil, and Satan.**

7. What nation was also called the Dragon in Revelation? **Pagan Rome**

8. What else falls under the umbrella of the Dragon? **Paganism, Mysticism, Spiritualism, Heathenism, Witchcraft, and their distant cousin, Astrology**

9. What does the sea represent in Bible prophecy? **Peoples, and multitudes, and nations, and tongues (Revelation 17:15)**

10. What does the Beast of Revelation 13:1 represent? **The Papacy**

11. Name the three animals that constituted the first Beast of Revelation 13. **Lion, Bear, and Leopard.**

12. Why does Daniel list these beasts in the opposite order that John the Revelator lists them? **Daniel lived during the time of the Lion and was forward-looking to the future. John lived in Rome and was looking back towards Babylon.**

13. When did Papal dominance begin and end? **538 AD - 1798 AD**

14. What nation represents the False Prophet? **The United States of America**

15. List the attributes of the False Prophet that determine what nation it symbolizes. **1) The USA rose to prominence after 1798, 2) The USA rose to prominence in the sparsely populated lands of America, 3) The USA served as a safe haven for those fleeing persecution in Europe, 4) The USA claims to be a Christian nation.**

16. What verse in the Bible declares the three in one aspect of the Dragon, the Beast, and the False Prophet? **Revelation 16:19**

17. List the three rules used to determine the meaning of 666.
    a. **(Rule number one – A man in Bible prophecy sometimes refers to a kingdom, nation, or political system.)**
    b. **Rule number two – Satan's kingdom consists of three parts that work together as one.**
    c. **Rule number three – If you are unclear about symbolism in Revelation 13, check to see if it's referenced in Revelation 17.**

18. What phrase connects Revelation 13:18 to Revelation 17:9? **Here is Wisdom**

19. What nations are represented by the seven kings? **Egypt, Assyria, Babylon, Persia, Greece, Pagan Rome, and Papal Rome.**

20. Which of the seven heads received a deadly wound? **Papal Rome**

21. Explain how time, times, and half a time calculates to equal 1260 years. **Time = 360 days, times = 720 days, half a time = 180 days**

22. Who is the eighth kingdom? **United States of America**

23. Who gave the Beast his power, seat, and great authority? **The Dragon**

24. Whose voice was given to the False Prophet? **The Dragon**

25. Explain the message of Revelation 13:18. **666 represents the Devil's trinity, which is the Dragon and Beast, and False Prophet. The dragon is represented in the sixth kingdom but is manifested in the seventh and eighth kingdoms. The message is the Dragon, and all his enterprises exist in all three world powers.**

26. Explain what Ellen White meant when she said, "I saw that the number (666) of the Image Beast was made up." **The Dragon, the Beast, and the False Prophet are each one component of 666. Once the Image Beast (The False Prophet) came upon the scene, it was the last component to make the 666-trio complete.**

TOPICAL INDEX

A
Adonikam, 18
Andreas Helwig, 22
Antichrist, 38

B
Babylon, 28, 31, 58, 62, 68
Beast, 17, 33, 42, 43, 47, 48, 50, 58, 60, 61, 62, 63, 81, 82, 83, 86, 87

C
Caesar Nero, 29
Crowns, 47

D
Dragon, 42, 43, 44, 45, 46, 47, 48, 56, 58, 59, 60, 61, 74, 81, 82, 83, 86, 87

E
Earth, 28, 43, 44, 47, 52, 53, 54, 68, 74, 75, 78, 81, 85
Egypt, 46
Ellen White, 32, 33, 34, 51, 59, 86, 87
Europe, 44, 54, 55, 56

F
False Prophet, 42, 43, 55, 56, 57, 58, 59, 60, 62, 81, 82, 83, 85, 86, 87
Flood, 47, 53, 54
Froom, LeRoy, 22

G
Gematria, 24

K
Kabbalah, 25

L
Luther, Martin, 87

M
Mankind, 30
Mysticism, 25, 26, 45, 102

N
Nebuchadnezzar, 31
Nimrod, 28
Numerology, 25

P

Pagan Rome, 45, 71, 83
Papacy, 49, 50, 51, 52, 54, 55, 69, 74, 78, 83, 84, 85
Papal Rome, 50, 54, 71, 74, 80, 82, 83
Pope, 21, 22, 23, 24, 51, 52

R

Rome, 28, 44, 45, 46, 47, 49, 50, 51, 54, 59, 71, 73, 74, 77, 78, 80, 82, 83, 85

S

Seven heads, 47, 48, 63, 68, 69, 76
Solomon, 18, 19

T

Ten horns, 47, 48, 50, 63
The Seventh Day Adventist Church, 19
Trinity, 40, 41, 62

U

United States of America, 55, 56, 76, 80, 82, 83

V

Vicarius Filii Dei, 20, 21, 22, 23, 24, 26, 87

W

Waters, 48, 63

www.ingramcontent.com/pod-product-compliance
Lightning Source LLC
Chambersburg PA
CBHW062022290426
44108CB00024B/2749